Exposed To Winds

Special Edition

Selected Poems by *Arthur O.R. Thormann*
(with an Appendix of Poem Excerpts)

Copyright © 1999 Arthur O.R. Thormann

Canadian Cataloguing in Publication Data

Thormann, Arthur O. R. (Arthur Otto Rudolf), 1934-
    Exposed to winds : selected poems

ISBN 0-9685198-0-6

    I. Title.

PS8589.H54945E96 1999   C811'.54   C99-900469-7
PR9199.3.T479E96 1999

Publisher: Specfab Industries Ltd.
Edmonton, Alberta, Canada

Printer: Quebecor Jasper Printing
Edmonton, Alberta, Canada

Cover Design & Photograph by Renate E. Thormann

To my wife...

...and my daughters,
...and our grandmothers and aunts;
...and to artists everywhere.

MY THOUGHTS

Life is full of enigmas, and millions upon millions of books have been written trying to explain them. Each of the books has achieved a small degree of success—some more than others. The degree depends upon the flow of the mind. As is so often the case in life, the door to baffling situations cannot be forced open. Only with rare, mental receptiveness can a few glimpses of the enigmas be obtained, and then only briefly—sometimes just for split seconds—and darkness takes over again. There are keys which can help one in such situations; one of them is simplicity.

Every time we understand a complex situation, we are awed by its simplicity. However, in the process of trying to understand it, our thoughts become more complex than is necessary. It is only when we return to simplicity that understanding prevails. This, in itself, is one of the enigmas of life.

Another enigma is the purpose of life as far as human beings are concerned. Some philosophers would have us believe that our purpose is no more than that of the lowest forms of life. Perhaps they are right, but our minds do not accept this; this is why we constantly strive to improve our situation. Lower forms of life do this too, of course, but not with the same degree of success.

To my way of thinking, the ultimate improvement of our minds is the spiritual one—the one that brings us closer to our maker. Some people reject this as fuzzy religious thought, and their only aim in life becomes one to improve their physical well-being. So be it! I think this is no more than what the lower forms of life are trying to do. We, as human beings, have been endowed to accomplish more, even more than mental improvements, and it saddens me to see so many of us reject this. We literally use up our lives to strive for mere physical improvements—improvements which are lost when life ends. It seems to me that even if there is only one chance in a trillion that our spiritual beings surpass those of our physical ones, we owe it to ourselves to go after it—develop it, as it were.

I sit sometimes contemplating life around me, and I see little that makes any sense, other than improving the physical and mental comfort. Even when I see half-hearted attempts at improving the spiritual life, it seems to me that it is only another way of improving the physical. Therefore, I conclude that people, by and large, have difficulty with this enigma. Perhaps they think it is too difficult to figure out or to accomplish, or that it is just that: an enigma, best left alone. They fail to realize the simplicity of it all, and it saddens me. I could go on in this vein, but enough said.

A few years ago, I tried to crystallize my thoughts on this subject, mostly for my own benefit, and I decided on the poetical form of writing—mainly because it is brief. I make no claim to its poetical accuracy—or to any kind of accuracy. It pleased me, and some of it pleased a few of my friends. If it pleases you, too, good! Otherwise, just ignore it. Truth is, after all, just another enigma: few people recognize it, or even want to recognize it, but if they do, even to a small degree, it shall set them free, of course. But none of us can become wholly truthful without becoming one with our maker: another enigma!

On the whole, I tried to portray life in all its wondrous facets. Most of my writing, having been done inspirationally, I don't quite understand myself. So, please don't ask me too many questions. Just get your own meaning out of it—related to your own experiences. If it works, fine! If not, just remember this: none of us can live each other's life. We must do it on our own! And we must seek understanding on our own, as well!

Arthur O.R. Thormann
Edmonton, Alberta
November, 3, 1994

INTRODUCTION

These poems came to me over a limited period of time: twenty-some years. They literally started in a blinding flash, then hailed upon me for some time and eventually petered out. I grouped them not chronologically but under certain section headings which I felt were appropriate at the time. Now, I'm less certain about categorizations.

Take my poem title *In The Beginning*, it does not really convey my true thoughts about the concept of *beginning*. There really is neither a beginning nor an end, I believe—there are only changes that deceive us into thinking in terms of a beginning and an end.

The title for this book I borrowed from one of my poems. I thought it was most appropriate because we are constantly exposed to winds, as it were—cosmic winds, if you like, that sweep across our souls for eons and eons, never letting up.

I wrote two or three poems of significance in the German language. I tried to translate these into English but finally gave up after I saw the translation inaccuracies of Goethe's poems. However, I believe that the gist of these German poems is adequately expressed in the present selection, so I decided to omit them. Albert Schweitzer once said that the German language is like walking through an enchanted forest. However, I find, in comparison, the English language is not lacking in this regard.

At the end of the book, I included an appendix of poem excerpts. These are memorable passages some readers might like, and this list will provide them with a handy reference to the poems from which they were taken. I also split the section and poem lists and put the poem list at the back of the book, to avoid a lengthy table of contents.

I sincerely hope that these poems will give you some enjoyment and plenty of food for thought!

SECTIONS

BIRTH   11

LIFE   17

LOVE   57

BEAUTY   69

FREEDOM   75

ENIGMA   87

DEATH   107

CONTINUUM   117

APPENDIX   121

POEM LIST   133

ABOUT THE AUTHOR   134

BIRTH

☺

Beginning or continuation?
As with death,
that is the question!

☺

IN THE BEGINNING...

I asked myself:
What's xodipusz?
What is it that's
Eluding us?

But no amount of
Questioning
Produced the slightest
Answering!

It was explained.
I thought again.
I pictured suns
I pictured rain:

It's wind with rage
It's storm that calms
It's tumbleweed
It's songs of Psalms:

It's gliding wings
And sometimes cries
It's coupling of
The dragonflies:

It's patient stones
It's woman's love
It's cooing of
A peaceful dove:

All that and more
Is xodipusz,
But it is still
Eluding us!

MY OTHER FACES

And yet another dream:
I'm in the land of the dead:
Awaiting my next mission.
My mission depends:
If somewhat successful,
I go on,
If not,
I stand still—or regress!

The whole process is like clockwork:
Nothing ever fails,
Nothing goes left
That should go right,
Nothing goes up
That should go down.
I think of favoritism,
But there is none!
I think of bias,
But there is none!
Progress or regress,
That is all!
Standing still is regressing.

I find myself praying.
Why do I pray?
I want favoritism!
But there is none!
God! What is this?
Why am I singled out?
But I am not:
There are others—
Others just like me!
I look at them
And I see myself!

Who are they, these others?
Why do they stare at me?
Because I stare at them:
I don't believe my eyes.

My name is called:
I get up slowly
And come forward.
The verdict is simple:
I have failed
In the land of the living!
I must return:
Better luck next time!
All my successes
Are merely recorded.

I'm fading away now.
And my other faces?
They only stare—
From a distance, mind you
With sadness, I imagine.
But in a flash
I can no longer distinguish them!
And I am reborn!

BACK ON COURSE

When we go astray, when we miss the mark,
We must pay to get back on course;
Sometimes it seems that the price is too high,
But balance demands this with force!

WINDMILLS OF YOUR MIND

As the windmills in the meadows
So the windmills of your mind
Turn the wheels of your existence
In a slow but steady grind.

IN SOLITARY HARMONY

The foregoing is the journey of a mind
That wonders, wanders, and meanders
In a quagmire of uncertainties,
Griefs, anxieties, loneliness,
And tension.

For such a journey to be peaceful,
The mind must become one:
With itself,
With its surroundings,
Its companions,
Its maker.

And yet, it must also stay detached,
For such is the law of the universe.
No amount of association,
Companionship,
Union,
Socialization,
Can change this universal law.

But much grief can be avoided
By being harmonious with all
Instead of a select few.

LIFE

Is it unfolding chemistry?
Biochemistry?
Or is it consciousness?
Cosmic consciousness?

DARK CLOUDS

The clouds loomed dark on the horizon,
As dark as an unlit nook,
And it should not be too surprisin':
They had an ominous look!

I watched them appear in the distance
Like messengers of some fate;
I watched, and I watched; with a sixth sense:
I watched them disintegrate!

I thought of my future with sadness:
There is always change for change:
And I wondered why not our gladness
Could take on a farther range!

I viewed the ominous clouds once more:
How easily they dispersed,
How insecure was their center core,
How flimsy and unrehearsed!

Perhaps this is so in our lives
With clouds of an unreasoned fear,
With threats that are caused by our strives,
Perhaps they will all disappear?

MANAGING LOSS

I went to school and made my grades;
I went to mountains and to glades;
I earned my share and spent a lot;
I think I valued what I got;
And all my life this nagging thought:
Does it have meaning more than naught?

In days of early youngsters' age,
When we lose toys and display rage,
We do not know that loss is life,
But we get trained to follow strife:
From kindergarten onto to school—
Get educated: that's the rule!

Our first loss might be some new toy,
Or bedtime, when we're full of joy,
Or our friends, when we change schools,
Or pride, when punished breaking rules,
Or curfew, when we have been bad,
Or mother's smile, when she looks sad.

As we grow older, loss is more severe;
We may lose much of what we're holding dear:
There isn't a moment in everyone's life
When loss doesn't overshadow his strife;
At every turn we're losing more,
And no one's there to total the score.

The score, and how we handle it,
Is what gives life its special wit;
Some drown in loss, and some emerge
With a new outlook, a new verge,
With a new reason for their strife:
Managing loss—That's our life!

SERVICE, PLEASE!

The other day, I travelled to
B.C.'s interior—to and fro.
I filled my car with gasoline
At seven stations—midgrade—green.

And then the thought occurred to me:
We're in a country—living free—
Where service stations do abound,
Where e'er we drive, one can be found.

Sometimes they do not have midgrade;
Instead, there's diesel—diff'rent shade.
But, by and large, the service' good—
Often you can get even food.

But do we thank those who invest
Both life and money at their best?
Seldom we ever give it thought—
We act as if it were for nought.

We take for granted everything
And expect service like a king!
One day, when service isn't there,
We get as angry as a bear.

And so we live our lives in shame;
Most our actions are in vain;
And when it's time to say good-bye,
We sit there staring at the sky.

We don't know what it was about,
Or why our rich life gave us gout;
We still expect others to serve,
And if refused we lose our nerve.

21

HUMAN NETS

One day I sat in a coffee shop
And watched a building rise;
The only things visible at the time
Were the steel beams and their ties.

And slowly my mind began to build
The outer façades of sheet,
And also the inner floors and walls,
Till the whole thing was complete.

But my mind took all apart again
Until only steel was left,
And the enormous sadness shaped itself
Till I felt I was bereft:

These monsters were nothing but human nets
Just waiting for us to fall
Into the traps that we didn't suspect
And thus they would catch us all!

How strong these nets were constructed, too,
How clever their designs!
That even their engineers were fooled
And failed to see the signs.

THE CRY AT NIGHT

When I must cry—I know not why—
I'll pick a night when out of sight
Of friend and foe who would not know
My inner grief—however brief.

I am not shy when thus I cry
The cry at night, and give no right
To men or mice to criticize
My inner grief—however brief.

And so I sob without the mob,
without my friends, or helping hands,
Who'd not defend nor understand
My inner grief—however brief.

With stars that shone I am alone
To contemplate my game with fate
And great desire to keep a fire
For need to grieve—however brief.

This stops with sleep that is not deep
But full of mares and frightened hares
Who would not fight or cry at night
With inner grief—however brief.

HEAVEN IS HERE TODAY

Some people slave throughout the year:
To have a holiday,
And others don't take holidays:
To put their cash away;
Most people work with blinding force:
To see results some day,
But many suffer needlessly
For carrots far away.

Their misery seeks all of those
that wish to join the team,
And thus the evil days are here
As trade-offs for a dream.
And when their dreams materialize
They're running out of steam:
Their attitude has worn them down:
They've lost that joyful gleam.

So suff'rers take a moment's time
And think of better ways,
Do not refuse what you have now
In hopes for better days,
Do not develop attitudes
That shut out daily rays,
Please recognize that heaven's here
Forever and always!

MINDS ASTRAY

We talk, we listen, we read engrossing books,
We wrestle with the problems of the day,
We esteem good music, poetry and looks,
And, we have curious minds that go astray.

When we listen to music, whether old or new,
We're appreciative, and sometimes gay,
Or, we are melancholy, if the tune is blue,
And few could convince us that we're astray.

How many "good" books do we read in vain?
And how many to find a new way?
How many books will provide us a gain?
And how many more lead us astray?

At times when we're busy with daily strife,
And we look for every warm ray
That can give new hope to a drabful life:
We don't realize we are astray.

We may find some cures for body and soul,
Or we may find a lot more to say
About what we all should have for a goal,
But we don't see us going astray!

UNISEX

Our trend is toward unisex,
Or uni-anything,
Equality's the slogan now,
In work and everything.
Some men play actress
And some women carpenter.
Some never know what's his
Or what belongs to her.

Nor does it seem to matter
That these differences prevail,
What seems the more important
Is that we should never fail.

Beauty only exists
Opposite ugliness.
A river only flows
If water sheds from crests.
Each North must have a South,
Each East a West,
Each tree must have its roots,
Each worst its best.

Where would we be
If hot and cold were gone?
Or black and white?
Or suns with dusk and dawn?
I think the universe
Would be a sorry sight;
But then, who cares it's dull
If we don't know what's bright?

Must we attempt to imitate so soon
A heat death certain to be our ruin?

STOPOVER

Have a liverwurst bread and a draft of ale
At Bermuda's Hog Penny Inn;
Get a feeling of new and a feeling of old
And a waitress who treats you like kin.

If it's stout beer you like or some good german food,
With herring in sour cream,
You have chosen a place where the sailor frequents—
A place resembling his dream.

Though the prices are fair, the old hog penny's gone
That the sailors had won when they raced,
And the island has changed its inhabitants, too,
There are no more hogs to be chased.

But the chocolate-brown lassie who brings you your ale
Is the friendliest thing you can meet,
"One-seventy, sah", is the small tab she makes,
With a smile that is nothing but sweet.

HARBOR OF REST

When the sails are full,
Though the sun's going down,
There's time, still, to be on the way
To a harbor of rest
And refreshments in town
And a short, but enjoyable, stay.

CULTURAL STARVATION

Cultural starvation is possible
In large countries and small,
In large cities and small,
In villages, and almost any crowd.

There's no enlightenment of tastes,
No intellectual training,
No aesthetic development:
Like living under darkest cloud.

The mind that's used to culture soon deforms:
It atrophies beyond the basic norms;
It shrinks in size and cries for help out there;
It agonizes night and day, what's fair?

The mind soon dulls to meet its counterparts:
Those who don't know the diff'rence in their hearts;
Those who are zombies to the world outside;
Those who take dullness in their daily stride.

And, strange enough, a happiness ensues:
A happiness that has no further use
Of cultural development of mind,
Or any other intellectual kind.

A fact that is not often understood:
Cultural downfall also brings some good:
The masses elevate themselves at its expense
And benefit from this turn, ever hence.

Small though this consolation to us seems,
We must remember what we owe our teams:
A team it was that gave us our train'
In culture that now seems to us in vain.

SHOW AND TELL

The poor man dreams of bettering his plight;
The rich man keeps his riches out of sight;
But the middle class displays his fancy things,
Be they his houses, sailboats, or his rings.

The rich man has no need for such display:
He is beyond pretense and poor's dismay;
He looks upon the middle with despise,
But this, too, he knows how to well disguise.

The poor man, he is envious, no doubt,
Of middle's pose as one who has the clout,
But after he has vented his disgust,
He looks at middle as one who is cussed.

And middle takes no note of all of this:
He walks around as if he's in a bliss;
The more he has the more he will display:
Oblivious to contempt and all dismay.

DESTINIES

If you think about leaving, you'll leave;
If you think about staying, you'll stay;
It is not good old fate
That determines this state
But the thoughts you nurture this way!

BODY AND DESIRE

A favored spot on the waterfront
Is the English Bay Cafe,
Frequented by natives and tourists alike
On just about any day.

And there I sat one afternoon,
Engrossed, at my window seat,
As the sailors raced their little boats,
And the surfers wet their feet.

Pedestrians rushed off somewhere,
And the traffic moved right along;
The seagulls cried their haunting cries,
And it dawned on me what was wrong:

No matter where I looked afield,
In open or hidden place,
I saw, controlled or uncontrolled,
The bodies of human race:

And for their bodies they slaved away,
Whether consciously or not,
Whether work, or play, or simple tasks,
They would slave until they rot.

I do not mean that it isn't fun,
Whatever they will do,
But whether fun or whether pain,
It is just a human zoo.

Because every act and every wish
Is for the body's sake,
Even their prayers ask for this,
In dreams or wide awake:

"Give me today my daily bread,
Oh Lord of high Esquire,
And forgive me all my trespasses:
For such was my desire."

THE ANTIQUE STORE

There is a tiny, junky store,
No more than a hole in the wall,
Where the junk has gathered from near and far
For sentiment's beg and call.

If you want to buy junk that's where you go,
And also when you sell,
So the junk is simply moved to and fro.
How often?...Who can tell?

Try picking the oldest junk you have
And take it to the store:
The owner will not even laugh—
He'll ask you yet for more!

The older the junk the more you pay—
It's a little bit like wine—
The higher the price the more you'll say:
This high price, it is fine.

The store is known to all the freaks,
Especially from far away:
Here is where we have stored antiques
For you to take away!

CAN'T THINK

And I travelled again at exceeding speed
Through the mind-boggling realms of computers,
But try as I would, on a scientific base,
I remained with the billion commuters.

At first I was scared, as the jack rabbit is
When he looks at the fox from a distance,
But I conquered my fear by sheer power of will
And the strength of internal resistance.

My progress was slow, and my concepts were wrong,
And the math I had learned was quite senseless;
I tried to solve issues by process of mind,
But my logic just left me defenseless.

The computer can't think, but nevertheless,
It can switch its circuits with speed;
If we input the slightest of nonsense to it,
We will soon regret our deed.

If computations are vast and inputs small,
Computers are time-saving friends;
But try to employ the opposite scene
And observe how fast friendship ends.

If the program we buy will fit our need,
We're fortunate in the extreme:
The alternative is a programming task
That will soon leave us wanting to scream.

The breakthrough we're striving and waiting for
Is a computer that can think:
The ultimate luxury we all want,
And the last of the missing link.

A link that can tie us to outer space:
To the mysteries beyond:
To universes as yet unknown:
To dreams of which we are fond.

HER GOLDEN AGE

We're here, today, to celebrate
Our loving mother's Golden Age;
We're happy for her healthful state
To help her enter this new stage.

A person's doing something right
When passing fourscore frozen times:
A struggle's seldom not a fight,
A poem's seldom without rhymes.

Our Angelita knows this well:
She fought off famine adm'rbly;
She lived through wars and peace and hell
And has not done so radic'ly.

We know she has no earthly wealth,
But she has wisdom without fears!
We wish for her continued health
And many, many happy years!

JOE THE FARMER

I have to tell you about Joe,
Joe Garner is his name,
He worked his way from spade and hoe
To farming as his game.

And farming he knows very well,
The weather notwithstanding;
He starts his day when most still sleep,
And all days are demanding.

He seldom takes a holiday
From the chores that are his life—
If it isn't seed then it is hay,
And he doesn't see it as strife.

He is not rich, as many think,
But he has everything that he needs;
It's his satisfaction that stands out,
And his richness is in his deeds.

All his Sundays are Thanksgiving Days
In the church he helped build for the Lord;
He shakes his head at the battles he sees
For he does not believe in the sword.

The wind has weathered the skin of his face,
And the rain has washed off his dust;
His hands are the paws of a man who works hard—
Every day he does what he must.

His product is sought by the rest of us,
But we do not give it a thought;
We do not stop to recognize
What this man's hands have wrought.

Thus are his days fulfilled by him
And his never-ending toil;
He digs his treasures year by year
From his yielding, willing soil.

And if he thanks the Lord for this,
The Lord He, too, sees him;
He smiles His sunny smile at his crop
So that it doesn't grow slim.

GROPING

In the darkness all around us,
Very little can I see,
And the light up in the heavens
Only more confuses me.

Give me fading stars above;
Blinding lanterns; sunshine, bright;
And you have not stilled my question
Where I'm going: is it right?

But there is a light within me,
Small, at first, and flick'ring weak;
Getting stronger by the minute:
Pointing out the path I seek.

Only when I look inside me
Do I know I'm on the track;
Do I know to go on safely,
Not desiring to look back.

THE BUSY HOUSEWIFE

She stands in line to pay for food:
There is boredom on her face,
There is also some anxiety
To continue with the race.

Her loved ones will be home real soon:
They'll want a decent meal,
No matter what the holdup is:
Their hunger is for real.

What's taking the cashier so long?
The line's not moved at all;
She is envious at number three,
Where the staff is on the ball!

Pay cash, rush home, put water on,
Scrub carrots, soak the peas,
Sear steaks, cut bread, set table, too,
All good things come in threes.

She knew the evening would be
The same as yesterday's,
The same as all the ones before,
The same in many ways.

Was this her lot of fate to be?
Was this why she was born?
The very thought frustrated her,
Invoked in her a scorn.

Enough of this philosophy!
Attend to soup and meat.
Forget these useless thoughts for now,
You must turn down the heat!

Oh woman of the greatest kind,
When will you ever learn
That everything that's made for thee
Is made for thee to earn?

She listened to her youngest one
Returning from a roam:
It'll only be five minutes now
Before everyone is home!

Her husband was the first to come,
And he poured himself a drink
To forget the trouble he was in
When a client made a stink!

After the supper: cleanup time,
While her loved ones watched TV,
If she hurries, she may catch a glimpse
Of a show worthwhile to see.

The demands were never ending,
As her loved ones snacked away!
At bedtime she made sandwiches
For lunch the following day.

The first one up at quiet dawn:
And another race begins!
With all her tasks she has some doubts:
Who loses and who wins?

Oh woman, do, please, take the time
For the cravings of your soul,
Lest years of toil and urgencies
Will take a heavy toll!

PURPOSE

We live for purpose, and it must be there,
Or else we are depressed and challenge what is fair.
In purpose there is power, so we're told,
And this is taught again until we're sold.

My purpose is my work, will many say,
And they will hardly rest on any day;
Yet others find their purpose in the books:
They live in schools and libraries and nooks.

Some farm, some fish, some raise the brood,
There is a purpose in most any mood,
Some build the boats, some sail, some just play ball:
When there is purpose, there's enough for all!

We measure purpose on a diff'rent scale,
Some seems worthwhile yet other's only frail.
Also, our thoughts vary a great amount:
One thinks a purpose high, other, of small account.

On one thing we can readily agree:
We must have purpose that we all can see!
The bum who lives his life without a goal
Is generally considered a poor soul.

It's possible that there is detriment
In purpose that will all but leave us spent:
Think of the time we waste for all of goodness' sake
With no thought that there might be more at stake.

Yet without purpose there is little life—
It seems that purpose goes along with strife—
Without a purpose most of us will live with stress,
But here, too, we need balance to have some success.

Great is the purpose that forgets the now
And questions all of future's where and how
Without ulterior motive in the mind:
The ultimate perfection for mankind!

AWAITING SPRING IN FALL

A howling wind sweeps over
Bending poplars: newly bare;
The wind comes from the North
With biting, wintry air.

The trees are a reminder:
Winter comes with little fuss;
It comes when least expected,
And it catches all of us.

Oh God! I hate this season
In all its cruel form:
When it shines, I'm out of shape,
And when it blows I'm in the dorm.

Through winter I look forward to
New spring in all its bloom;
In the meantime, I am stuck here,
At the window of my room.

QUALITY VS. QUANTITY

The aim today is longevity:
To live to eighty and more;
Nobody is happy with brevity:
It's as if we must reach a high score.

But the life each of us leads
Is full of waste:
Nobody takes stock of his deeds,
And his deeds are performed
In neck breaking haste,
As if he had no other needs.

And so our desires are secular:
For the highest of quantities;
We often sacrifice by far
All the better of qualities.

As long as quantity is there,
We do not question the price:
We assume that everything is fair,
And we do not look at it twice.

You cannot balance poor quality
With an increase in the amount:
It is best to forget about quantity
When you balance this type of account.

That's why your moments must be the best,
For they never improve being stretched:
The many times you put this to the test,
You will usually end being wretched.

Try being prepared
For the briefest of stays
Without being scared
To run out of your days.

Longevity, if not put to good use,
Is worse than the shortest life lived,
Especially if we manage to lose
Our claim to this one-time gift!

MOTHER

A mother's love is sure to never fail;
A mother's never sick when loved ones ail;
A mother's ears are tuned in when she sleeps;
A mother is who tears when loved one weeps;
A mother is the sun that shines at rain;
A mother is support without a feign;
A mother's job continues when we're done;
A mother has to work when we have fun;
A mother is the love that doesn't fade;
A mother is the tree when I need shade;
A mother is concerned when all is well;
A mother is who burns when I'm in hell;
A mother is the stem that holds the rose;
A mother is the friend I never chose;
That's why we're very pleased to say
These things to her on Mother's Day!

FOOLISH INVESTMENTS

Succumbing to attacks
Of temporary greed,
We invest in many things
That we soon no longer need,
We waste resources
And we waste our time
Without much thought
Or reasoning or rhyme.

We overeat, we overdrink,
We oversleep and overwake,
We overestimate ourselves
And say a lot "for heaven's sake",
We answer little
And we question less,
And then we wonder greatly
Why we're in distress.

We pay a lot for doctors
And, still, we're always sick,
We consume a lot of drugs
But none will do the trick,
We think we need a holiday
So we fly off to some isle,
Then we lie around on beaches
And get bored to death in style.

We invest in houses,
Bonds and common stocks,
We buy ourselves some rings
With big, expensive rocks,
We build a lot
And tear a lot more down,
When one of us says "stop",
We kill him with a frown.

Tomorrow we shall do
What must be done;
Tomorrow we shall stop
This foolishness!
Tomorrow we'll get serious:
To hell with all this fun;
Tomorrow we will earn
Our heaven's bliss!

EXPOSED TO WINDS

My life is hard
I hug the ground,
And dust is my companion.
Your odious life,
I'm told by some,
Is useless in the ending!

Lo...I gave might,
Improved the sight,
And built the towers skyward;
I wasn't first,
And won't be last,
But my need is universal!

From stone to dust
I alternate,
And my cycles are eternal;
Exposed to winds,
No friends to love,
I live my life in silence!

43

NOT DARING IS FATAL

I have a friend who's now a member of AA,
Upon a time he lived in horror and dismay,
To join up was a major step he took—
At times he doubted with a backward look.

The step that took enormous will and daring
Brought him a life of openness and sharing,
And suddenly his friends were many more
Than seashells in the sands of any shore.

His love for others once was nonexistent!
Nor did he care if he was inconsistent:
His stories were as wild as he at times,
And people laughed at him more than his rhymes.

The only friend he'd left was his poor wife;
She hardly coped with him and other strife!
One day it came to blows and she lost out:
One thing she couldn't cope with was his clout.

That was the straw that broke the camel's back!
He cursed himself for having such a knack
As always choosing wrong from left and right:
It mattered not if sober or if tight.

After this final turn he searched and then he found
A better way of life that turned him all around;
Not only did his mental outlook change,
But also found his spirit newer range.

And, so, his soul improves from day to day:
No longer is his life one of dismay;
No longer is he fighting with himself;
No longer needs he bottles on the shelf.

NEVER EVER NEVER

Some things I feel like doing;
Some things I'd rather not;
Some things agree with me
And others turn to rot.

I could have saved my organs
A great deal of abuse
Had I not done the things
That hurt them to amuse!

I'm never ever able
To give a clear-cut "No"
When well-intentioned signals
Will warn me to go slow.

My life's most likely shortened
And full of ill-timed stress
As my mind and soul succumb
To all my weaknesses!

BALANCE

We're afraid of imbalance
Since our numbers grow high,
And we may not have food
But dust in the sky;
Our cities grow larger—
Our farms disappear;
But behold:
There cannot be imbalance!

We fight good with evil
And evil with good;
Most religions try hard
To make it well understood
That individuals will perish
Unless saved from themselves;
But note:
On the whole, there is balance!

We pollute air and water;
We threaten the fish;
We kill off the animals
Not only for dish;
We diminish the trees
To print infinite trash;
But again:
There is only a balance!

We deplete our resources;
We change scenes where we can;
We divert our rivers
More to the liking of man;
We build here a new mountain
And there a new lake;
And still:
There is a new balance!

46

The change we create
May not suit us too well;
Our every-day wishes
May turn out to be hell–
But what seems like upset
Should nevertheless
Be viewed
As a new form of balance!

We overindulge
In what seems like a waste;
We cannot accomplish
Too much without haste;
We fret and we anger,
We storm and we fear–
And yet:
We again find a balance!

We gaze at the heavens,
The planets, the stars,
We send men to the moon,
And perhaps soon to Mars,
To explore what is different
From down here on Earth–
But everywhere:
There is a balance!

DECEIVERS

Misleading statistics
As tools of logistics
Can fool optimistics
And foul strategistics
As well as scholastics.

WHAT IS CHRISTMAS?

Is it sending cards off to your friends,
Or phone calls with merry wishes?
Is it giving gifts of latest trends,
Or turkeys and dirty dishes?

Is it colored lights and lit-up trees,
Or groups of early carnations?
Is it drinking rum sweetened by bees,
Or visits with your relations?

Is it jingling bells out where it snows,
Or songs from your record player?
Is it making peace with all your foes,
Or into church and a prayer?

Is it paying heed to Jesus Christ,
Or is it all worthless labor?
Is it what the senses has enticed,
Or is it "loving thy neighbor..."?

STRESS...REDUCED

I sometimes think:
This rat race is too rough;
I sometimes think:
Get out, you've had enough;
But if I must restrain
so stress can be reduced,
Where else to learn this
but where stress will be produced?

SUBTLE TRANSFORMATION

Striving for perfection,
Trying to be, every day,
What one is not,
Can be very stressful,
Can create subtle changes,
Due to stress
Going unnoticed,
For a time,
Before taking its toll.

TOO BUSY

I'm usually too busy to do
What I don't want to do,
And I'm never too busy
For all of my priorities!
But sometimes I'm sad
When the world thinks I'm mad
And when the time
I have on my hands
Is much too short
For all of my friends.
It is surely no excuse
When the time I put to use
Is only for priorities
Excluding all amenities.
There's more...but I'm too busy!

LUIGI'S

Luigi's is that happy place
Where warmth and friendship meet:
A cozy spot along the coast
Where wine comes with the meat.

Celebrities and folk alike
Feel romance in the air;
The southern wind is very mild;
The sun's extremely fair.

The favorite sport is windsurfing,
Some swim and sunbathe, too,
Some sail a Solo to and fro,
Some paddle a canoe.

At lunch: a salad from the sea,
With light wine from the host;
The conversation is alive,
With here and there a toast.

After the lunch: a quiet time—
You leave the sunrays be—
The cool rooms give a restful scene,
With an outlook on the sea.

After siesta: cocktails fizz,
And plans are made to dine:
Luigi's is the best there is,
And everyone says, fine.

What will it be then? asks a friend,
Lasagna? Fettucini?
Luigi's Special's favorite, too:
Scampi au Scallopini.

Let's have some wine, another says,
A dry red Folonari;
Another wants a sweet Vermouth,
A third, Asti Spumante.

And so the evening proceeds
With wine and dance in swing:
Romance is at its very best
As the tenor starts to sing.

Far into night they celebrate
Until the pairs retire,
But some will stay up very late
To hug a cozy fire.

One must experience Luigi's
To be fully in a trance:
Some say it's where it's located,
Others claim it is romance.

OUR GUESTS

Our guests are precious to us!
And while they are our guests,
They become part of us!
Whether in joy or in sadness,
We are one with them!

HELL'S BOREDOM

Sometimes I feel inadequate,
And I don't know why:
Is it my lifelong job?
Or, is it pie in the sky?
It's an interesting job,
And I know it well:
So, why am I bored?
And why is it hell?

Sometimes I think I'm getting old,
But the thought isn't fair:
My heart is still with it,
And it's not my gray hair;
Besides a few aches,
I'm otherwise well:
So, why am I bored?
And why is it hell?

At other times I'm just plain sad:
I feel I should cry!
Everything I examine
Is ready to die!
I want it to prosper,
And I want it to sell:
So, why am I bored?
And why is it hell?

A few times my religion lacks,
Or so I think.
Should I join a group
And get onto its rink?
I live better alone
Than on what people sell:
So, why am I bored?
And why is it hell?

And finally I watch the end
As if it's near!
I have done my best
And can live without fear.
You can start the countdown,
You can ring the bell,
But I am still bored,
And it is still hell!

VALUES

Some values stay around and others go,
Some increase and some decrease over time;
It's personal and relative, if so,
Oft not explained by reasoning or rhyme.

If time evaporates the interest
And familiarity the value of a fad,
The question that arises is,
"What must I do to keep from being sad?"

It matters not if things or thoughts or friends:
Importance fades, as high noon fades the sky;
We usually find reversal of the trends
And values lost to us as time flits by.

I seek a thing or friend or timely thought
Of lasting value, to maintain my strength,
Ignore those that can easily be bought,
And search for others over lifetime's length.

THE GOLDEN THRONE

I

The world must change and I shall do my best
To rearrange the norm and stamp out every pest—
    What went before is obviously fake,
    If not an outright, foolish, sad mistake!

I've learned my lesson and I've learned it well:
    I'm now equipped to 'radicate this hell;
My liberties are sanctioned by my country's law,
Which is the only thing we have without a flaw!

    Don't criticize my work or else I'll quit!
    Your tenure is not strong, from where I sit;
        I'll take a job up north at higher pay,
        And if you want to match it, I may stay.

The world owes me a living, that's for sure!
    Too bad nobody's ready for my cure:
These fools will once be sorry, be it known,
Just wait till I have built my golden throne!

    When all else fails, I'll travel as a bum:
        Exposing evils of the upper scum!
    I'll show the world that has neglected me
    That I still have the best philosophy!

II

    As I get older I am more and more alone,
And less and less attractive is that golden throne
    For which I longed in early, blooming years,
When life was full of hope and void of nagging fears.

    It's trivial now to think of all my strife:
    I've buried most of those who were my life:
For those I know the longest, I'm no longer there,
For those I meet today, it's hard for me to care.

And so I wander on my chosen path
And shrug a shoulder at my fellows' wrath:
Today it rains and in the morrow: shine!
The sorrow's emptiness will soon again be fine.

Man never knew the meaning of it all—
We're always strongest just before the fall,
And what seems bleakest and gives us the biggest fright
Looks different in the day than in the dark of night!

We would do well to look at failure's face
After we run and not before the race:
Do what you can and let the chips fall where they may,
You know you did your best: there'll be another day!

III

I see the balance now: a marvel of design:
What climbs today will once again decline—
Nothing's for naught and nothing's overly profuse
If once you understand its purpose and its use.

Our knowledge is so limited in sphere
That all we comprehend is now and here;
To know eternity's as folly to pretend
As knowing where beginning meets its very end!

And our values are no less distraught:
It is because we never have been taught
To put humanities ahead of things
That are the precious life of queens and kings.

Possess for pleasure but remember: it's a game!
Do not forget: you'll leave as naked as you came—
So feast your spirit and give all you can
To help your brothers and the lot of man.

When I look back on life I'm moved to tears:
I could have reaped some fruit in early years—
I've wasted precious time as I have sown

The useless seeds in striving for that golden throne.

IV

Do we obey design and universal laws?
Or do we sooner break the pattern with our flaws?
This is the subtle test to which we must submit,
And which expediency would rather have us quit!

FORGETTING TO REMEMBER

If I could remember far enough back,
I would, of course, find the source of my life,
But, as it is, I'm preoccupied with
Possessions, obsessions, and daily strife.

And what happens if I can't remember?
Do I miss my opportunity?
Must I repeat my search again
And repeat it for eternity?

Or can I ask for help somewhere:
A shining light, perhaps, within?
Is there a key that locks the door
That will not let the blind man in?

But the more my mind is obsessed with living
The more my memory fades away,
And eventually I may forget the search
Just living my life from day to day.

LOVE

♥

*The yearning and longing
of every shred of mind and body;
the resistance to separation;
the oneness with all in the universe...*

MY FRIEND

I have a friend who knows me well,
Who does not sleep when I'm in hell,
Who laughs with me and cries with me
And builds my ego constantly.

I have my times when blows of fate
Kill all my love and nourish hate,
And just when all looks dark as night
My friend is there to put things right.

At other times my heart elates:
I feel as if there were no hates,
And when I shout and sing my song
My friend makes sure I won't go wrong.

We sometimes talk of deeper things,
Of future joys and gatherings,
And always with a helping hand
I get some guidance from my friend.

As life proceeds my values change,
My thoughts find new and farther range,
But that which always will remain
Is our love that links the chain.

OH, MOUNTAIN, HOW I LOVE YOU!

Mountain, you look overpow'ring
And I love you!

Mountain, you threaten me
And I still love you!

Mountain, you move in on me
And I keep loving you!

Mountain, you are suffocating me
But my love is unimpaired!

Mountain, you have overpowered me
And all that remains is:

My love for you!

WISH FOR LOVE & HAPPINESS

May the rain provide you water
May the sun provide you heat
May the mountains give you pleasure
May you never know defeat
May your friends be true forever
And your enemies be rare
May you always find a person
For whom you may wish to care
May you live with all your neighbors
In the greatest harmony
May your love for one another
Be a joy for all to see!

THE HAPPY COUPLE

Two people searched, two people found,
A happiness which gave them ground
To join in wedlock their two souls
And plan their lives with common goals.

Their wedding was that merry feast
Where gloomy thoughts occur the least—
All guests had confidence regained
That happiness can be obtained.

And everybody wished them well,
Since life is still a struggle;
Forever did they want to tell
Of the very happy couple!

Yet wish for, search for, try to give
The happiness for which we live,
Will be an exercise in vain
And cause unnecessary pain:

Since happiness is but a state
Of mind which one must cultivate,
And grief can move in very swift
When love lets hate produce a rift.

And so, in ignorance of this,
Both our lovers went amiss—
Now, singly, they'll attempt to find
To which together they were blind.

YOU'RE A FAKE

You're a fake at heart,
Where I can't see your desires,
Where your secrets are in dark
And your passions little fires—
But I adore you!

You're a fake at heart
When pretending what you're not,
When you're hiding in the dark,
When pretending what I'm not—
But I adore you!

You're a fake at heart
When you sing your song of love,
When you whisper in the dark,
When you murmur like a dove—
But I adore you!

You're a fake at heart
When you say I'm more than you
And your thoughts remain in dark
So your charities are few—
But I adore you!

You're a fake at heart
As your love goes out to all,
And your prayers in the dark
Try to keep me from my fall—
But I adore you!

You're a fake at heart
As you whisper in my ear
To pretend it's never dark
Just to overcome my fear—
But I adore you!

You're a fake at heart
When you tell me I must yearn
As I travel through the dark
Feeling certain you'll return—
But I adore you!

AWAKENING

One day I sat in a mountain lodge
And watched the rain come down;
And as the clouds moved low to touch,
I could only envision their crown.

And my thoughts went deeper inside of me:
A place of eternal delight;
As my spirit sang a sad melody,
The rain drizzled down on my right.

The rain: she was a gentle mist,
Such as never does any harm,
And what she touched was merely kissed
By her gentle, disarming charm.

And as the sun burned through the mist,
The drops still fell from a tree;
And the steam arose from the gently kissed
As my mind returned to me.

ENAMORED BUILDINGS

And I had visions again:
Visions of trees growing inside buildings,
Visions of entwined boughs,
Leaves that passionately tried to touch,
Roots that grew up, out of the ground,
Vainly trying to hug the boughs:
The trunks were paralleling in close proximity,
Embracing themselves at the roots;
The tops whispered their songs of love,
And the air was charged with ions:
It could have been the garden of Eden,
Except for the buildings!

Then there was water: much water!
The water ascended in different channels
And descended in various ways:
Some came gushing down in waterfalls,
Some diffused into spray at the top of fountains,
Some formed clouds, some mist, some rain drops,
And in the midst of it all:
The most beautiful rainbow:
A rainbow only seen before in nature:
Never inside of buildings!

There were also benches:
Many benches in the middle of flower beds:
On the benches: lovers!
Lovers tightly embraced from head to toe!
They were motionless and silent,
But they appeared very real and alive:
Depicted were all great lovers
Since time immemorial!
Eden would have been idyllic for it, of course,
Only the buildings were out of place!

FISHER'S LOVE

After sea lions vanished to cool off in caves,
Our fisher heaved ho! on the oars:
His boat pointed seaward on sun-heated waves,
And soon he did not hear the roars.

At Sandy Point's shallows, five miles from the shore,
He tossed out the cuts of his bait;
Then lowered his nets, as he had done before,
And anchored his boat for the wait.

Forlorn and benumbed he rocked with the sea:
His eyes had a tale-telling gleam:
His first love, he thought, a beauty was she!
Enthralled he was lost in his dream.

And the night was upon him—he noticed it not:
His thoughts were still haunting the past,
But at sunrise he stirred, and he took hold the knot
To haul in his nets straight and fast.

The catch was too meager to take to the dock
And the nets more brittle than he;
He suddenly knew he had run out the clock:
Yet his love ne'er would set him free!

Refrain:
Fisher: Your nets are old and need much mending;
Oh Fisher: Why don't you pack it in?
Fisher: Your catches do need some defending;
Oh Fisher: You can no longer win!

THEIR LEADER

The North Pacific's where they roamed:
That grayish herd of whales,
And how they honored Tuskertou
Is strange among the tales.

'Twas Tuskertou that led them south
To their favored breeding ground;
'Twas Tuskertou that led them north
To toss and turn around.

'Twas Tuskertou that found them food
When finds were small and slim;
'Twas Tuskertou that stood his ground
When enemies looked grim.

'Twas Tuskertou that took the watch
When everyone was gay;
'Twas Tuskertou that spotted boats
Of whalers far away.

'Twas Tuskertou that faced a storm,
With the rest of them alee;
'Twas Tuskertou that taught their cubs
Survival in the sea.

When Tuskertou was old and weak
And finally doomed to die,
His followers revered him much—
Pathetic was their cry.

'Twas Tuskertou that was the first
To recognize the truth,
But he wanted to make one more run
To the beaches of his youth.

As they arrived along the shores,
The sun was hot and high:
It would only take a day or two
For their skins to be too dry.

But their love for Tuskertou was great,
And they didn't leave his side
Even after he was dead and cold—
At the mercy of the tide.

ETERNAL BOND

My wife, my life,
My thirteenth rib,
What would I do without you?
I'm sure you know
What this song tells
And how I feel about you.

We part by day
But bring at night
Our weary souls together:
In acts of need,
In acts of love,
And hopes that never wither.

The troubles that
We share each day
Form bonds that make us stronger
And give us both
A oneness that
Will last a lifetime longer.

THE PURGE OF LOVE

Love, pure, is the catharsis of the soul,
Not love of mate, or love of things or gold,
But global love should be our strongest goal:
The love that loves thy enemy of old.

The soul becomest one with all there is
When love prevails and conquers hate each day,
There is no question as to hers or his:
It's everyone's in every thinking way.

There is no question as to who can kill,
Or whom to kill and whom to let still live;
These questions are not answered by the will
But by the love that each of us can give.

It's useless to gain power as to rule
Without displaying love to underlings,
For very soon one ends up as the fool
That treats his fellows as if they were things.

Nor is the wisdom we may gain of use
If used in ignorance of love each year:
Most things we know just serve us to confuse
The reasons why we live and why we're here.

The things that make us rich here are in vain
When love is missing from our daily strife,
Since in the end we're only left with pain
And with a feeling of a wasted life.

For when the soul leaves this abode anew,
It should be carried on the wings of love;
Be it the love of many or of few,
The soul should fly as lightly as a dove.

BEAUTY

Δ

*To open up one's store
and let a spilling mind
demand one's soul
be fully bared...*

Δ

THE WORLD OF MUSIC

Sometimes I listen to a melody

And I hear music:

Each turn of the melody

Generates another:

There seems to be no melody

Which is alone:

Each melody has individuality

As well as multiplicity:

Each melody has joy

And also sadness:

Each melody presents

A separate world:

The world of music!

THE HORIZON'S SUN

Whether at dawn of morn

or at dusk of night,

The horizon's sun

is forever a sight

That grips at the heart

of the young and the old

Like the beauty of love

that is to unfold.

NATURE'S WAY

My eyes behold the beauty of this mountain:
The whiteness of its head that makes it seem
Like misty pearlings from a giant fountain
That fall between these rocks to form a stream.

I always longed to be a part of it:
A part of nature's secret beauty form:
A form devoid of all of human's wit:
A wit required to establish norm.

It isn't that the human beauty fails
Or that it's lacking in creative ways;
Nor that it has a want for fine details
Or works that have developed from a haze.

It's mostly artificial, nonetheless,
Unless the artist with that rarity:
That ultimate achievement of his bliss:
Released his mind to set his talent free.

Some artists have, as will their works reveal,
But there are very few, and far between,
Most are enslaved by how we others feel,
By quick rewards, and how they may be seen.

Again my gaze is resting on the mountain:
Again the simple nature of it speaks,
Nay, whispers, as the trickling of a fountain,
Serenely from the edges of its peaks.

STRANGE ATTRACTION

One last look at the alp
in the distance—
We leave longing and full
of resistance:
Still pulled by its beauty,
We heed our duty,
But already we plan
Our next trip!

FREEDOM

☼

The choice to dig a hole
and bury one's self,
and the choice not to.

☼

BAREFOOT IN THE STREET

When I was young I scorned the world,
With much I disagreed;
My mind revolted at the scene
And begged me to be freed.

At first I sought the company
Of intellectual friends:
A folly, I soon recognized,
That led me to no ends.

And soon my friends were shunning me
In public and alone;
I do not mind, I told myself
In a self-supporting tone.

But disappointment nagged my mind
Awake and half asleep;
My jobs got scarcer every year,
And I couldn't earn my keep.

The only friends that I had left
Were buddies in the bar,
And when I struck acquaintances
I lied, I'm from afar

And soon I walked in shabby rags
With nothing on my feet;
I walked through heat and rain and storm,
Just barefoot in the street.

And soon my hair turned white as snow,
There was little more to see!
My spirit's saddened over time,
But my mind remainest free.

BEACHED FOREVER

As may happen to us all sometimes:
I was shipwrecked on the rocks
In a strange, exotic, faraway land,
Where the waves that pound the beach
Recede each time with the shifting sand:
Now near, now out of my reach.

I, myself, felt like the shifting sand
Since I capsized in the sea:
I was stranded in this lonely bay,
In rags, and sick to my heart;
I felt I could never find the way
To make yet another start.

I don't know why I felt this way,
And why my feelings got worse!
With sunny skies and natives around,
I had little to complain:
All that I wished for was abound—
But my logic was in vain.

I did not dare to admit I found
A utopia in disguise:
It was freedom that I lacked the most:
The freedom to leave this place!
It was useless to explain to my host
That I felt myself in a maze.

And days turned to months and months were lost,
And so was many a year!
My mind was terribly atrophied;
My self: listless and forlorn—
Had my fate for me been prophesied
I'd wished I'd never been born!

Ev'ry day I wondered if someone'd spied
A ship from the far-off seas;
The natives silently looked at me:
How could they understand?
How could they know how I loved the sea—
How I loved that other land?

But inside I knew 'twas only me:
The enemy we must all fight!
While some of us do very well at it,
Others perish, yet they try!
Some do it with remarkable wit,
And some relent till they die.

PEACE

"Peace" says a lot!
More so than "health"
And "happiness",
More so than *"bon voyage"*,
"Peace" says you're one
With all there is
At every new *étage*!

THE CYCLE OF LIFE

And the powerful salmon rose fast from the deep
Towards shore and the mouth of the river;
She instinctively knew that her task could not keep,
Since her insides had started to quiver.

It was nearly five years since she'd left the big stream,
And a lifetime had passed in the making;
The attraction that'd forced her to follow her dream
Was fulfilled to the last bit of taking.

What a fight it had been, for the dream to be free:
A life's struggle that took her companions!
She remembered it well—the migration to sea—
And the rushing through darkest of canyons.

The rocks and the boulders, the sand and the silt,
Provided less food than the plains,
And she and her friends had consumed without guilt
Their mothers' and fathers' remains.

Farther down they were feasting on minnows and flies,
But the perils were never without:
Birds of prey came adiving right out of the skies,
And the anglers mistook them for trout.

When finally some of them did reach the sea
They were worn out and tired from fright;
They believed they had paid the price to be free
And imagined it would end the fight.

How saddened they were when a fierce enemy
Forced anew and continuing strife,
And they soon realized that nothing was free:
It was all in the cycle of life!

THE ARTIST

She combines her dexterity, talents and skill
With a soul-searching trip that is rare;
She reaches beyond the realms of the sane
To enclaves that had never been there.

She's yearned for release of her feelings for years
In a world that is full of pretense;
Whenever she thinks she's unravelled herself
She is told that she does not make sense.

Enthralled by the marvels released from her store
She is ready to let it all spill
And produce a new record engraved in a tape
That can't be erased by man's will.

She uncovered the latest of strange, hidden worlds—
Only seen with an eye of her own—
Pretenders delight, but the critics are mean,
And the ignorant leave her alone.

She may have long gone on her travels abroad,
Through the space of unlimited sphere,
When her works will receive some attention from those
Who were tied to a motionless pier.

PROGRESS

Progress everywhere!
But what is progress?
One has no sooner gripped
the romantic past,
and progress takes it away!
Progress is hygiene: Mr. Clean!
But is it?
Progress is pollution:
Pollution of air, water, space,
minds, and souls.
Progress is that which leaves me behind:
The faster it moves, the behinder I get.
Progress claims constructivism.
But it also destructs:
Our buildings, our surroundings,
our values, our gods.
And what is constructed
will soon be destructed:
That is progress!
Sometimes, not often, progress destroys:
It atomizes materials, concepts,
values, gods.
When this happens,
utter desolation follows,
and no further progress, construction,
takes place.
Ideally progress frees:
Frees the mind, the soul, the spirit.
A free spirit progresses faster,
and, thus, becomes freer and freer.
Nothing can hold it back,
except tradition:

Tradition conserves, preserves,
enslaves the spirit,
most often, puts it in regression.
Progress is the statue of liberty
for all spirits seeking freedom.
No such spirit is fully understood
by the enslaved, the encapsuled,
the traditional spirit.
Hail progress!

TO BE FREE TO BE

When I look at the birds,
I, too, want to fly;
I, too, wish to be free
To glide through the sky!

Sailing through life
When the wind is strong,
And another birthday—
How can I go wrong?

A LIFE OF SPONTANEITY

Do laws of states give liberty?
Or is it subtler, deeper kind
Of state that rules us, sets us free,
Gives satisfaction to the mind?...

As birds fly north and find their way
To nesting places for their young,
They follow instincts night and day
And never think of songs they sung.

When searching daily for their food,
No thought of shortages can dim
The mind to cause a fearful mood,
Although their pickings may be slim.

And ride the wind and chirp a song
And build a nest and look for worms:
Never a thought of doing wrong—
Take cover only when it storms.

Protect their young; defend their space:
It's all a part of daily strife—
No hurrying to win a race,
Or sorry brooding over life.

Thus raising young if shine or rain
And feeding plenty for the treks,
When lastly they fly south again
To leave a winter in their backs!

THE AIMLESS WANDERER

Every day of my existence,
Positiveness frightens me—
Let the leaders lead the losers,
And I wander aimlessly.

Time I have but precious little;
Knowledge I have not to give;
And I should not part with wisdom
Making me competitive.

When my vote opposes many,
And my efforts go astray,
And I must conform to others:
I get dizzy with dismay!

Do not offer me protection,
Since it bothers me to share
When my interests differ widely
From the ones who claim to care.

Through my shyness I'm neglected;
Socialness suppresses me;
I don't want to be a member—
Let me wander aimlessly!

MIND SEDUCED

To strongly influence a person's mind
Can easily estrange him from his soul:
His thoughts are not his own, and you shall find
His acts will soon betray his former goal.

This is the curse of every tyranny
That seeks its fortune in a dictator:
His is the only mind that still thinks free,
And every stooge becomes a self-traitor.

Insidious is the force that spreads about,
Diseased the thinking that cannot escape
The pattern set by him who has the clout
And hesitatest not to do his rape!

Control the mind: control the passions, too,
His loves, his hates, and also his ideals:
His actions all take place without a clue
To tell him who controls the way he feels.

And, so, his course continues without guilt,
Without the slightest thought of doing wrong;
His borrowed strength is built up to the hilt:
The only weakness is his faith that's wrong!

ENIGMA

∞

Some call it religion...
some call it enlightenment...
others simply live by it!

∞

THE SUPREME EXISTENCE

I had a dream
And the dream was most enlightening...

And in the dream
The supreme existence was perfect!
And, being perfect,
It had no real existence,
For real existence
Is always imperfect...

But the dream revealed
A perfect concept,
And in the concept
Manifested good and evil:
For good and evil
Are but two sides
Of the same coin...

And the dream further revealed
That the supreme existence
Was at once
Central and divergent:
Being central,
It proved its surreality,
For it was so perfect
As to tax fantasy:
And being divergent,
It embraced all of reality,
For it permeated
Everything in existence...

And in my dream,
I begged to become one
With the supreme existence,
For I was overcome
With awe and joy...

A GENTLE RAIN

Dining one day at the Jasper Lodge,
I'm looking at misty shades of green;
At drizzle of rain out over the lake;
At a very somber but restful scene.

The rain makes me think of cleanliness;
Of never-ending cycles to endure;
Of gentle washings of the rocks and trees;
Of comfortable dryness, to be sure.

The rain that falls is not destroying things;
Is not uprooting plants, or breaking them;
Is not removing soil where needed most—
Just rocking flowers lightly on their stem.

I'm prone to dream at so much gentleness;
Such splendor of a very fruitful kind;
And I am lost in perfect, peaceful thought
When Goethe's wisdom starts to stir the mind:

The human soul is like a gentle rain:
It comes from heaven and returns thereto
And down to earth once more and up again,
Forever alternating—to and fro.

THE TENTACLES OF GOD

When God wanted experiences
Akin to earthly strife,
He came to create tentacles
Known as the human life.

He then gave homo sapiens
A wondrous, sacred soul
To tie him to the universe
In fulfilment of this goal.

God also gave the human soul
The freedom of his choice
To live a life of misery
Or live it to rejoice!

Now, all of these experiences
Arc welcomed by the Lord,
But His laws will also let us know
What we can ill afford.

There're those that lose and carry on
And those that will succumb;
this is the test designed for us
For missions still to come.

ETHEREAL JOURNEY

Their faces: beautiful and sad:
Sad multitude that stared at me:
Their movements and their haunting sound
Evoked reminders of the sea.

A sea that rolls eternally
With rushing sounds upon the beach;
A sea that holds the mermaids fair:
Forever out of our reach.

It is not often that we see
Their faces floating on the waves;
More seldom, yet, we have a chance
To follow them to secret caves.

They swim like dolphins having fun,
And on, and on, their movements turn;
Their eyes are big, and sad, and wet,
And when they look at me, I yearn.

Forlorn I sit upon the beach
And let the waves engulf my feet;
My heart is out there with the maids;
My spirit's singing with a beat.

Just as the sea, my sadness rolls,
And my emotions rush at me;
My fibers tingle at their ends;
My eyes are blank and do not see.

And soon my being is engulfed
By waters of emotions torn
Between realities and dreams,
And soon I feel I'm not yet born.

And so I drift through time and space,
Through galaxies and milky ways,
Through worlds that never have been seen,
Through ether winds of future days.

The sea has calmed, the maids have gone,
I look around with saddened eyes:
Nothing of what I saw remained—
The stars are normal in the skies.

THE MISSING LINK

Oh xodipusz! Oh xodipusz!
What is it that's eluding us?
I went to school; I went to work;
I ate; I played; I wept; I slept;
I went to church; I prayed to God;
I've had my toil; I've had my fun;
I think I did what should be done;
I think I have an even score;
And yet, I feel like doing more!
I think and think and think and think
And cannot find the missing link!

THE LAW

Father of the universe,
mother of humanity,
Please hesitate before you
perform miracles for me—
For miracles are nothing but flaws—
Help me, instead, to obey your laws.

Be it known that your laws are perfect,
And, being perfect, they're also strict,
And, being strict, they won't set me free
to live life with utmost liberty.

Both, good and evil, both, love and hate,
Are subject to laws that some call fate!
So why do I continually ask
For miracles to reduce my task?

When I should be asking to understand
What has been put here and governs our land,
I whimper, instead, like a little child,
For things to be easy and very mild!

I should be seeking that unity
That creates nothing but harmony!
Instead, I have become the slave
Of that which earns an early grave.

THE ONE AND ALL

I am the One...I am the All...
I am who saved you from your fall!
I'm here, I'm there, I'm everywhere,
And it is *you* for whom I care!

You look for me in oddest places
And do not recognize my faces,
But I am there for you to see,
And my secret is...*Simplicity!*

I'm where it shines and where it hails,
I am the Law that never fails!
At times, what seems like chaos is
Subject to rules which *cannot* miss!

Unbending though my rule may be,
You are a short time from it free;
But to save you from eternal loss,
I've built a bridge for you to cross!

I am the One...I am the All...
I am the Tall...I am the Small...
I am who waits you patiently
To cross the bridge..to join with me!

NAKED IS THE SOUL

Naked we come, naked we stay, naked we go:
Naked in body, in mind and in soul.
However much we hide our shame,
We will always stay the way we came.

The body can be clothed, the mind disguised;
The soul stays naked, often, too, despised:
Each truth and falsehood does with ease appear
For all to see after the now and here.

Sometimes the soul is mirrored in the aging face,
Just as it mirrors oft the origin of race,
But this is not indicative of much,
Since no appearance is the soul as such.

It is the soul that wanders to and fro—
No sooner here, it readies self to go—
And so it reaches heights where no one's been,
Yet, it is good its bareness can't be seen.

There'll come a time when all souls can remain,
When to and fro will not have been in vain,
When bareness will not be to someone's shame,
When naked will not serve a musing game.

THE PATH

As oceans roll their waves across the waters,
As icebergs show their peaks and hide their bulks,
As clouds move on and rain goes through its cycle,
As water turns from ice to liquid, vapour, and then snow,
As stones roll down the sloping mountain sides,
As stars track in their universal orbit,
As engines mesh their gears and turn their wheels,
As grass and shrubs and trees grow taller and then die,
As birds soar high and dolphins roam the depths,
As men and women live their lives for play or toil,
A reckoning proceeds without perception:
A universal law that governs all:
It is the law of balance, you must know,
Which never rests nor leaves a debt unpaid!

Transgress the limits and prepare to pay the price –
Whatever you will take must be returned:
Be it a grain of sand or half a cup of rice!

And I remembered Henry Miller's words:
The path is the same for God as for man,
For the vegetable as for the star.

Amen!

FAITH AND TRUTH

And the Lord looked upon His peoples
with sadness,
For there was much confusion:
His peoples had lost the faith,
And without the faith they were unable
to recognize the truth!

And the Lord decided to send a messenger;
The messenger had to be trustworthy,
Lucid and determined,
For there was much confusion!

But the messenger was truly bewildered,
For he had never before encountered
such confusion.
Also, he was conscious of
his grave responsibility,
And he begged the Lord to come to his aid.

And the Lord reassured him in earnest
And brought home the matter's
graveness and urgency!
And the Lord's messenger set out on his mission
To clear up this great confusion.

And he spoke to the peoples with clarity
and determination!
And all the peoples heard
but did not listen,
For in their confusion they had lost the faith,
And without faith they could not
recognize the truth!

And the Lord looked upon them with sadness!

WHAT IS TRUTH?

If you have ever pondered over truth
And answers did not readily appear:
Do not despair, but nourish faith:
And truth will come, since it was always here!

Truth is the balance of the universe—
It cannot lose a part without a gain—
And those who seek a profit with no loss
Will spend a lifetime at it—all in vain!

Each south has north—each pole its counterpart—
To find the truth one must assume the right
Of viewpoints opposite to one's own heart
And readily accept without a foolish fight.

One truth is truth means diff'rent things to us:
Each person sees it changed with his own eyes:
Each person thinks the world is in a mess
And seldom knows himself to tell the lies.

Truth challenges the open mind of all—
To recognize a falsehood is an art—
Changing opinion at a moment's call
Can best be done with pure and open heart.

Truth also favors those who are naïve:
Who have the faith beyond reality:
Who constantly express their own belief
In right that adds up to totality!

To walk the narrow path that leads to truth
Is sometimes awkward and oft filled with pain,
But those who tread the path in solid faith
Will find their search for truth was not in vain!

FROM ZERO TO INFINITY

All through my younger years I was obsessed,
Obsessed by concepts of divinity,
And two such concepts which my mind had pressed
Were the unknowns of zero and infinity.

To think of zero is to think of not a thing:
A feat I found impossible to learn:
I strained myself until my ears began to ring,
And in the end I left myself to yearn.

By "zero" I don't mean dividing points
Between the pluses and the minus sides,
Or precise centers of revolving joints,
Or where the frozen waterform abides.

And by "infinity" I don't mean very huge,
Or quantities immense in their amount,
Or waters covering Earth a long time in d'luge,
Or numbers much too large to give us count.

Not only are these concepts hard to comprehend,
Especially with such undetermined state—
One has no beginning, the other has no end—
But, also, neither leads us to a gate.

These concepts may escape us, yet, eternally:
One is a void the other one is space:
One's zero, and the other is infinity:
And neither can be caught up in a race.

Again'n'again, at fast and at exceeding speed,
I travelled throughout the spaces galore,
And, yet, there was no way to let myself be freed
From the feel I had of being ashore.

IMAGO

Gradually, there was a yearning:
Our attractions grew stronger and stronger;
Our virtues were accentuated,
And we were blinded to our faults.

Our beings were fused,
And we became one!
It was like a dream.

We were in never-never land,
And it didn't seem real:
Like the land of love, of lovers.

But at times it appeared real:
Everything was illuminated, elucidated.
It could have been reality
If it hadn't been a lie!

THE AGELESS MIND

If you can think of one huge mind,
You have the human race,
Which pulses with regularity
Behind an invisible face.

And as it throbs it swells in size,
This mind of enormity:
It's forever anti-tie-me-downs
And anti-conformity.

In a free state it will thrive and thrive,
It will add to development;
It's appetites are always there,
Never settled, never content.

It's ambitions, too, are limitless,
With the universe its field;
No obstacles can hold it back,
No excuse provide a shield.

And every human adds to it,
In whatever minute way;
The human body shrivels up,
But the mind is here to stay.

And so it grows through age and space,
Through war and holocaust;
It's true size is a mystery,
But we do know it is vast.

Some go so far, they think it's God,
This faceless human mind,
But others don't believe in this:
Their god's a diff'rent kind.

Regardless of the point of view
That some of us may hold,
We do not recognize the truth
Until we're much too old.

And yet, age is irrelevant
To the mind of human race:
Each part is like a dying cell
In an never-wrinkling face.

It is replaced immediately
By fresh cells of a kind
Which 'juvenate and generate
This ageless human mind.

SINCEREST WISH:

Oh, Great One:
Let me be one with Thee:
Let me be one with myself:
Let me be one with my fellow men:
Let me be one with the universe:
I beg this of Thee!
Amen!

JUSTICE

I called the devil and he came!
(Later I thought it was a shame.)

We shook hands, and he appeared like a friend
But his eyes were as hard as his bony hand.

His charming smile is what fooled me the most;
He was also courtly and a very good host.

When he asked for my soul, I didn't mind:
He was like a father and very kind.

I, too, have asked him for many things,
And he never denied them (as strange as it rings).
One day I asked him for a real big favor:
I wanted justice for me to savor!

But he shook his head and smiled with glee,
"It's not justice you want", he said to me,
"For justice you have already got,
Or is it so long that you forgot?"

He looked at me as if amazed,
And I looked back: my eyes were crazed.

I was filled with terror and wanted to run,
But he poked at me in jovial fun:
"Don't let it get you down my friend,
I am still with you, here, take my hand".

And in a daze I took his hand:
It was as warm as that of a friend.

After that the one thing I never wanted
Was more of the justice that has me haunted.

I COME AND I GO

You try to kill me with excuses;
You also try some drugs on me;
But I'm immune to these abuses,
And I come and go regardlessly!

Sometimes I cause severest pain,
And it hurts me when you suffer,
But I hope your trial is not in vain—
Otherwise...It could get rougher!

How often have I heard it said?
"Go away!" and "Do not bother!"
But I come when you not wished I had,
And I watch you like a father.

I am your conscience day-night long
Many turmoils have I battled!
I come when something rights you wrong,
And I go when you have settled!

RETURN!

Return, you gods of separated boughs,
Return to us and exercise your vows,
Stop outward swing of our pendulum,
Return to us an equilibrium.

THE NAGGING DOUBT

When we are young and our dreams are big,
The world is just ahead:
All we must do is only reach
To take the rosy bed.

And as we near our journey's end,
We view it with some doubt:
There should have been some meaning there!
What was it all about?

And oft we think that our lives
Are worthless ere we die;
It might have been a truism
If it hadn't been a lie!

Wee do we know less understand
That all was just a test—
Let life take its mysterious course,
And let us do our best!

DEATH

☹

Leaving, but for a moment,
an emptiness:
a space that someone's occupied...

☹

TIME, THE GREAT ENEMY

We're told that cells deteriorate with age:
That nonrenewal causes us to die:
That this is so if rich man or if sage;
We're told it is a law we can't defy.

But it is time that kills us, not our cells:
Time is the enemy that we must hate:
Time is the stream of sand that never gels:
Time is the wax that truly seals our fate.

The faster time goes by the sooner we arrive
At our destination: far or near;
At last we're led to wonder why we strive
And why we're put to struggle now and here.

If we could only make the time stand still,
Much progress would result without the ties
That time imposes on the human will,
Which tapers off and breaks before one dies.

Instead, we're told that time continues on
Without a break and at an even pace:
Continues on long after we are gone:
Continues fast, whether we loaf or race.

Eternity suggests time has no end—
Incomprehensible to our human mind—
A concept we may never understand
As long as we remain with our kind.

That's why it is important that we choose,
Without much bother and without much fuss,
To break away from time before we lose:
To free ourselves from bonds imposed on us.

GRATIFICATIONS

I decided on a holiday—
I'd earned it (so I thought)—
I was looking for a quiet bay
Where lodgings could be bought.

I found a spot near the eastern coast
With a climate warm and mild,
And lodgings with a very good host:
I was as happy as a child.

I savored all the gourmet foods
And enjoyed the local wine;
The music added to my moods:
What a perfect place to dine!

I sunned myself plenty during the day,
Or I strolled through the old part of town;
There was never a reason for dismay;
There was never a reason to frown.

At night I walked along the beach
And breathed in the ocean air;
The stars no longer were out of reach,
And God and fellows seemed fair.

And romance was in abundance, too,
All in clean, good-natured fun!
Without romance, who'd know what to do?
Who'd feel anything should be done?

But all good things must end one day:
A law we all forget—
One last look at this quiet bay
With feelings of regret.

GENE'S GIFT

Gene's dead?
All know when someone's died
He leaves, but for a moment,
An emptiness: a vacant space
That he himself had occupied.

Not Gene!
There was no emptiness,
No fading, dwindling thought,
No rush of flowing rivers
From pining depth of sorriness.

Gene's 'live!
He went where no one's dared
To open up his store
And let a spilling mind demand:
His soul be fully bared.

That's Gene!
The fullness of his life,
The throb of his vitality,
His song, his laughter, all of him
Still cause of our lesser strife.

A TEAR FOR A FRIEND

When you lose a friend
if by death or by deed,
A friend who was faithful
in sorrow or need,
A person whose friendship
was never decreed,
You are tearful.

Mere thoughts of a loss
that might never occur,
The witness of sorrow
emotions can stir,
To suffer ideas
you cannot deter,
Makes you fearful.

You may ask for the whys
or shrug it all off,
You may bleed inside
yet your outside is tough,
Feeling sorry for self
can be very rough,
You're not surest.

But a friend who is dying
can render your heart
As sore as the flesh
that is pierced by a dart,
For once you are tongue-tied
and no longer smart:
You feel helpless.

Your heart is a throbbing
and tenderized sore,
You want to reach out
and touch him once more.

But the distance' too great
and the silence' a roar:
You are strengthless.

And yet you must face
a much greater design,
Where losses lose meaning:
it's not "yours" or "mine"
Where a oneness prevails
that you cannot align:
It's the purest!

THE ARROWHEAD VINE

It grows!
Adds leaves...
by one and one...

But look!
The first...
it withers, shrivels, dies:

The cause?
Who knows...
its rhyme or wit?

Just age!
It seems...
the same for all applies:

It's earth!
Of course...
that must be it...

LORD! TELL ME THEY NEED KILLING!

We hunt the bear, we hunt the deer,
The sport is very thrilling,
And when the season opens up:
Lord! Tell me they need killing!

At times when our lust and leer
Caused woman's womb a swelling
And no one wants the embryos:
Lord! Tell me they need killing!

There are some bugs that give us fear,
Their numbers are still growing,
And when they spite us constantly:
Lord! Tell me they need killing!

Then there's a war that rages here,
My brothers bide the calling,
And when the enemies come strong:
Lord! Tell me they need killing!

When villains torture us with jeer
And burn down our dwelling,
And when they murder, rob and rape:
Lord! Tell me they need killing!

We have these criminals each year
To whom death is compelling;
When nothing else will hold them back:
Lord! Tell me they need killing!

"You have instructions that are clear
And require no more telling!"
But Lord! When all is said and done:
I still think they need killing...

A PEOPLE LOST

Some lie, some cheat,
Some murder and some steal,
Some get caught and stop,
And some repent,
While others still continue:
Their lives are like...
A river that meanders.

Some play too much,
Some overeat,
Some drink, some smoke,
Some change their trend,
And some remain oblivious:
Their lives are like...
A river that meanders.

Some love themselves,
Some love their mates,
Some love their neighbors,
And some love hate,
Some go to church,
While others like to sleep:
Then lives are like...
A river that meanders.

Eventually they die
And drop to bottom:
Like silt that swarms the ocean...
By the millions:
One drops on top of others
And others on top of one:
Thus ends...
The river that meanders.

KILL ONE:
AND A THOUSAND COME TO BURY IT

Insignificant, though, the mosquito is,
It, too, is endowed with a measure of bliss;
It, too, likes to eat and to sleep and to dance;
But we shouldn't permit it as equal a chance.

We should not admit that it, too, has a life;
It, too, has to struggle to follow life's strife;
It, too, must consider its efforts defeated,
Unless it can see its life's cycle repeated.

We should rather assume it has power of mind
To maliciously calculate acts so unkind
As to pester us constantly morning and night,
With little regard for our nerve-racking plight!

...Having thus been created an enemy strong,
We no longer consider it awfully wrong
To do what is obvious that it be done
To continue our lives in undisturbed fun.

CONTINUUM

↗

...but never The End!

↗

THE CONTINUUM

Ashes to ashes,
Dust to dust,
Such is the path
Of the living;
And the new birth
Of ideas,
Such is the path
Of eternal life!

THE JOURNEY

Sometimes, the human mind
goes on a journey:
A journey that lays bare
and exposes its vulnerability...

A journey that shows it
the joys of life
and the many griefs
of its struggle...

A journey that brings
no rest...

A journey that has
no end...

Mine is such a journey...

I'LL JOURNEY ON...

I'll journey on
My task is done!
I've travelled well
Through heaven's hell.
To stand this trial
Was worth my while:
I've learned to live
And love and give.
I do not leave
to give you grief—
I have to go
And help you so!
But in my heart
I'll only part
To join with thee
For eternity.
Now do not cry
And ask not "why?"
Go seek and find
To which we're blind!

APPENDIX

Subsidiary, perhaps,
but not to be confused
with secondary!

⟺

POEM EXCERPTS

As we grow older, loss is more severe;
We may lose much of what we're holding dear:
There isn't a moment in everyone's life
When loss doesn't overshadow his strife;
At every turn we're losing more,
And no one's there to total the score.
[20]

◊

Some drown in loss, and some emerge
With a new outlook, a new verge,
With a new reason for their strife:
Managing loss—That's our life!
[20]

◊

Most people work with blinding force:
To see results some day,
But many suffer needlessly
For carrots far away.
[24]

◊

Beauty only exists
Opposite ugliness.
A river only flows
If water sheds from crests.
Each North must have a South,
Each East a West,
Each tree must have its roots,
Each worst its best.
[26]

◊

And for their bodies they slaved away,
Whether consciously or not,
Whether work, or play, or simple tasks,
They would slave until they rot.
[30]

◊

He is not rich, as many think,
But he has everything that he needs;
It's his satisfaction that stands out,
And his richness is in his deeds.
[34]

◊

Only when I look inside me
Do I know I'm on the track;
Do I know to go on safely,
Not desiring to look back.
[35]

◊

Oh woman, do, please, take the time
For the cravings of your soul,
Lest years of toil and urgencies
Will take a heavy toll!
[37]

◊

On one thing we can readily agree:
We must have purpose that we all can see!
The bum who lives his life without a goal
Is generally considered a poor soul.
[38]

◊

Try being prepared
For the briefest of stays
Without being scared
To run out of your days.
[40]

◊

Succumbing to attacks
Of temporary greed,
We invest in many things
That we soon no longer need,
We waste resources
And we waste our time
Without much thought
Or reasoning or rhyme.
[42]

◊

My life is hard
I hug the ground,
And dust is my companion.
Your odious life,
I'm told by some,
Is useless in the ending!
[43]

◊

I could have saved my organs
A great deal of abuse
Had I not done the things
That hurt them to amuse!
[45]

◊

It matters not if things or thoughts or friends:
Importance fades, as high noon fades the sky;
We usually find reversal of the trends
And values lost to us as time flits by.
[53]

◊

The world owes me a living, that's for sure!
Too bad nobody's ready for my cure:
These fools will once be sorry, be it known,
Just wait till I have built my golden throne!
[54]

◊

I see the balance now: a marvel of design:
What climbs today will once again decline—
Nothing's for naught and nothing's overly profuse
If once you understand its purpose and its use.
[55]

◊

Our knowledge is so limited in sphere
That all we comprehend is now and here;
To know eternity's as folly to pretend
As knowing where beginning meets its very end!
[55]

◊

If I could remember far enough back,
I would, of course, find the source of my life,
But, as it is, I'm preoccupied with
Possessions, obsessions, and daily strife.
[56]

◊

I have my times when blows of fate
Kill all my love and nourish hate,
And just when all looks dark as night
My friend is there to put things right.
[59]

◊

You're a fake at heart
As you whisper in my ear
To pretend it's never dark
Just to overcome my fear—
But I adore you!
[62]

◊

The soul becomest one with all there is
When love prevails and conquers hate each day,
There is no question as to hers or his:
It's everyone's in every thinking way.
[68]

◊

The things that make us rich here are in vain
When love is missing from our daily strife,
Since in the end we're only left with pain
And with a feeling of a wasted life.
[68]

◊

When I was young I scorned the world,
With much I disagreed;
My mind revolted at the scene
And begged me to be freed.
[77]

◊

She may have long gone on her travels abroad,
Through the space of unlimited sphere,
When her works will receive some attention from those
Who were tied to a motionless pier.
[81]

◊

Every day of my existence,
Positiveness frightens me—
Let the leaders lead the losers,
And I wander aimlessly.
[85]

◊

To strongly influence a person's mind
Can easily estrange him from his soul:
His thoughts are not his own, and you shall find
His acts will soon betray his former goal.
[86]

◊

The human soul is like a gentle rain:
It comes from heaven and returns thereto
And down to earth once more and up again,
Forever alternating—to and fro.
[90]

◊

God also gave the human soul
The freedom of his choice
To live a life of misery
Or live it to rejoice!
[91]

◊

I should be seeking that unity
That creates nothing but harmony!
Instead, I have become the slave
Of that which earns an early grave.
[94]

◊

You look for me in oddest places
And do not recognize my faces,
But I am there for you to see,
And my secret is...*Simplicity!*
[95]

◊

The body can be clothed, the mind disguised;
The soul stays naked, often, too, despised:
Each truth and falsehood does with ease appear
For all to see after the now and here.
|96|

◊

Transgress the limits and prepare to pay the price—
Whatever you will take must be returned:
Be it a grain of sand or half a cup of rice!
[97]

◊

If you have ever pondered over truth
And answers did not readily appear:
Do not despair, but nourish faith:
And truth will come, since it was always here!
[99]

◊

Truth is the balance of the universe—
It cannot lose a part without a gain—
And those who seek a profit with no loss
Will spend a lifetime at it—all in vain!
[99]

◊

If you can think of one huge mind,
You have the human race,
Which pulses with regularity
Behind an invisible face.
[102]

◊

Regardless of the point of view
That some of us may hold,
We do not recognize the truth
Until we're much too old.
[103]

◊

I am your conscience day-night long—
Many turmoils have I battled!
I come when something rights you wrong,
And I go when you have settled!
[105]

◊

And as we near our journey's end,
We view it with some doubt:
There should have been some meaning there!
What was it all about?
[106]

◊

If we could only make the time stand still,
Much progress would result without the ties
That time imposes on the human will,
Which tapers off and breaks before one dies.
[109]

◊

And romance was in abundance, too,
All in clean, good-natured fun!
Without romance, who'd know what to do?
Who'd feel anything should be done?
[110]

◊

Some play too much,
Some overeat,
Some drink, some smoke,
Some change their trend,
And some remain oblivious:
Their lives are like...
A river that meanders.
[115]

◊

POEM LIST

A Gentle Rain 90
A Life Of Spontaneity 84
A People Lost 115
A Tear For A Friend 112
Awaiting Spring In Fall 39
Awakening 63
Back On Course 15
Balance 46
Barefoot In The Street 77
Beached Forever 78
Body And Desire 30
Can't Think 32
Cultural Starvation 28
Dark Clouds 19
Deceivers 47
Destinies 29
Enamored Buildings 64
Eternal Bond 67
Ethereal Journey 92
Exposed To Winds 43
Faith And Truth 98
Fisher's Love 65
Foolish Investments 42
Forgetting To Remember 56
From Zero To Infinity 100
Gene's Gift 111
Gratifications 110
Groping 35
Harbor Of Rest 27
Heaven Is Here Today 24
Hell's Boredom 52
Her Golden Age 33
Human Nets 22
I Come And I Go 105
I'll Journey On... 120
Imago 101
In Solitary Harmony 16
In The Beginning... 13
Joe The Farmer 34
Justice 104
Kill One: And A Thousand ...116
Lord! Tell Me They Need ...114
Luigi's 50
Managing Loss 20
Mind Seduced 86
Minds Astray 25
Mother 41
My Friend 59
My Other Faces 14
Naked Is The Soul 96

Nature's Way 73
Never Ever Never 45
Not Daring Is Fatal 44
Oh, Mountain, How I Love You! 60
Our Guests 51
Peace 79
Progress 82
Purpose 38
Quality Vs. Quantity 40
Return! 105
Service, Please! 21
Show And Tell 29
Sincerest Wish 103
Stopover 27
Strange Attraction 74
Stress...Reduced 48
Subtle Transformation 49
The Ageless Mind 102
The Aimless Wanderer 85
The Antique Store 31
The Arrowhead Vine 113
The Artist 81
The Busy Housewife 36
The Continuum 119
The Cry At Night 23
The Cycle of Life 80
The Golden Throne 54
The Happy Couple 61
The Horizon's Sun 72
The Journey 119
The Law 94
The Missing Link 93
The Nagging Doubt 106
The One And All 95
The Path 97
The Purge of Love 68
The Supreme Existence 89
The Tentacles Of God 91
The World Of Music 71
Their Leader 66
Time, The Great Enemy 109
To Be Free To Be 83
Too Busy 49
Unisex 26
Values 53
What Is Christmas? 48
What Is Truth? 99
Windmills Of Your Mind 16
Wish For Love & Happiness 60
You're A Fake 62

ABOUT THE AUTHOR

Arthur Thormann was born in 1934 in Berlin, Germany. His grandfather emigrated to Canada in 1930 but didn't have enough funds to take his entire family with him, not even his wife. Little by little, over the years, he brought his sons, his wife and finally his daughter, Arthur's mother, and her children to Canada. They arrived in 1951.

After the traumatic experiences in Germany, Canada was a welcome haven. However, Arthur, who had his first training in Berlin as a precision instrument mechanic, found no job in his field. After spending some time on farms, in machine shops and as mill mechanic, he took a retraining as an electrician and managed an electrical construction company for a number of years.

He has always had a keen interest in the literary arts and has published, himself, over the years, many articles on various topics. His favorite hobby, however, was to express his observations and philosophies in some poetic form, a form that pleased mainly himself but also, occasionally, his friends and relatives. It is they who asked him to consolidate his poems in one book. He and his wife have made their home in Edmonton, Alberta.